Random Curves for a Fruitful Life

LIFE IS A TREASURE HUNT

Dr. Tamiko Smith, MBA

Random Olives for a Fruitful Life: Life Is a Treasure Hunt
© 2021 by Dr. Tamiko Smith, MBA

Random Olives for a Fruitful Life is a trademark of Bicicletas En Brunch, LLC.

For information, contact: Bicicletas En Brunch, LLC
BicicletasEnBrunch.LLC@yahoo.com

For information about bulk book orders, downloads, eBooks, and to request Dr. Smith for speaking engagements, please contact Fulfillment Services at BicicletasEnBrunch.LLC@yahoo.com.

Editing, design, and production by Backspace Ink (www.backspaceink.com)

Image credits from Shutterstock.com: Looker_Studio (cover and copyright page), bierchen (page 13), sophiablu (page 15), Eddie Lepp (page 17), TheSaif (page 19), Gustavo Frazao (pages 21 and 23), inacio pires (page 25), Anant Kasetsinsombut (page 27), Michelle Patrick (pages 29, 31, 71, 83, and 91), By Ditty_about_summer (pages 33 and 63), Wiktoria Matynia (page 35), marekuliasz (pages 37 and 89), rawpixel.com (page 39), Bicicletas En Brunch, LLC (page 41), Leon T (page 43), Nikki Zalewski (page 45), Oleg Podzorov (pages 47 and 73), GreenLandStudio (page 49), inxti (page 51), Anton Evmeshkin (page 53), Khakimullin Aleksandr (pages 55 and 81), Maksim Shmeljov (page 57), cdrin (page 59), cherezoff (page 61), Steve Wood (page 65), Gts (page 67), Kichigin (page 69), Lidiya Oleandra (page 75), Andrey Grigoriev (page 77), agsandrew (page 79), Comedstock (page 85), vor (page 87), Bandolina (page 93), TypoArt BS (page 95), TTstudio (page 97), Lightspring (page 99), Illya Kryzhanivskyy (page 101), Fishman64 (page 103), amasterphotographer (page 105), Razoomanet (page 107), and Svetlana Kononova (page 109).

ISBN: 978-0-578-79003-9

Printed in the United States

Don't be afraid to go out on a limb.
That's where the fruit is.

—H. JACKSON BROWNE

Thanking my grandmother, parents, and sisters
for always inspiring and loving me!

*L*ife is a treasure hunt, and *Random Olives for a Fruitful Life* takes you on a self-help journey. Each poetic motivational quote will tap into your quest for healing and push the limits to live outside of the box.

In your life, you will hit roadblocks, barricades, and brick walls that try to impede your growth and limit the drive to be your authentic self. As you move through this book, you will gain a sense of inspiration and empowerment. I have used my unique social encounters, travel experiences, and reflective memories to develop thought-provoking windows of opportunity. Hopefully, these examples will promote a zestful change in your lifestyle.

Throughout *Random Olives for a Fruitful Life,* you will discover simple ways to freely "move about the cabin" and gain more insight about the things that make you feel fulfilled and adventurous.

Feel free to use the left side of the page of each poetic motivational quote as a vision board. Post on …

Contents

Explore Range of Emotions

GROUNDED SANCTUARY

Download *Under the Tuscan Sun*
Keep this on standby as well:
Eat, Pray, Love
Select a vintage James Bond flick while you are at it

Take a Chance

FEARLESS COMFORT

Travel to the South of France
Take a bus from Marseille to Côte d'Azur
Cohabitate in a loft with a friend
Pursue a carafe of rosé and some occasional French fries
Cook fresh Mediterranean fish, mussels,
XL tiger prawns with haricot vert
Rise early in the AM to music and fresh fleurs
Fetch a fresh baguette with splendid olive oil
Feel free to double dip

Rhythmic Travel

SOUL ENRICHMENT

Listen to some old-school music:
Phyllis Hyman
Angela Bofill
Womack & Womack
The Emotions
Candi Staton
Phil Collins

Pick an unknown artist
Replenish

Orchestrate Your Life

UPLIFTED SPIRIT

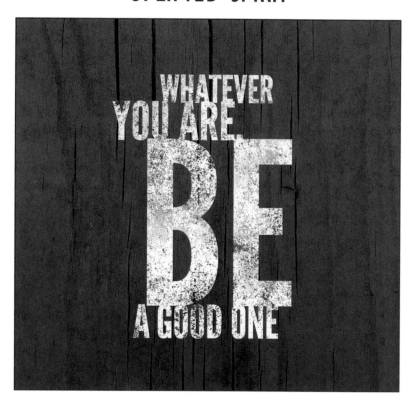

Start with Diana Ross's "Love Hangover"
Spend $40 playing a TouchTunes jukebox in a dive spot
Take requests
Be open

Predictability Yields Boredom

VALIDATE COURAGE

Take day trips and make them different
Allow the local grocery store trip to be an escapade
Try a different aisle for a start
Create small wins

Recreate Old Memories

SOOTHING LAUGHTER

Text a high school friend
Laugh about memories
Pick out yearbook pictures with funny hairdos

Create a Fruitful Life

RANDOM OLIVES

Unplanned attendance at a local wine social club
Order a flight of wine with ash goat cheese
Chat with a person next to you
Share the experiences of your palate

Initiate Small Victories

RANDOM OLIVES FOR A FRUITFUL LIFE

CONFIDENCE BUILDER

Get a new recipe offline: Pinterest
Try it with friends
Even share with your coworkers
Try again

Never Stuck

CHANGE VENUES

Download Pandora
Be endless with your music station choices
Think outside the box

Don't Be Shy

EUDAIMONIA

Send a thank-you card
Show your appreciation for a new friend
Take your time making your card selection
Reflect on the message you're sending

Cleanse from Within

REFRESHING BEGINNINGS

Drink a crisp, dark blue bottle of spring water
Splurge a little
Choose more than one if you desire
Cleanse your emotional well-being

Self-Affirm

APPRECIATION OF LIFE

Do
more
of what
makes
you happy

Text a daily affirmation
Press "send" to yourself
Feel the pulsating vibration
Awakened

Exceed Expectations

RANDOM OLIVES FOR A FRUITFUL LIFE

PURPOSE

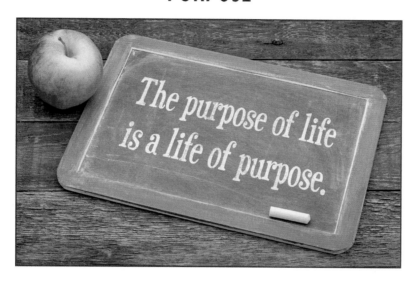

Travel to Tenerife
Enjoy the beaches on the coast
Enjoy a mixed green goat cheese salad while poolside
Order Chinese food in Spanish

Relinquish Control

BE A GUEST, NOT A HOST

Fly to Milan
Ride the #19 bus
Take a train to Firenze
Get invited to a nice stranger's house
Perch at an authentic wooden table
Fresh veggies, blended meats, and artisanal cheeses
Enjoy the pleasantries
Stay inspired through travel via Hey Lady™

Be Optimistic

LIVING HAS NO PLACE FOR BOREDOM

Barbecue on a cool winter's day
Fuzzy boots and a warm jacket
Add a new spice to your life
Get lost at the Portobello Market

Blended Expectations

SAVORY MOMENTS

Choose mixed Mediterranean olives
Accented with stuffed blue cheese
Opt for salmon basted in pistachio oil
Extend your comfort zone
Indulge in Sugar Pills podcast
Self-care affirmations are in abundance

Take a Step Back

NO MORE NEUTRAL

Play Scrabble, Connect 4, and Uno
Catch up to your hidden childhood memories
Put it in reverse
Heal beyond Chutes and Ladders

Always Stay in Motion

RANDOM OLIVES FOR A FRUITFUL LIFE

RELATIVITY

Take a walk in Rittenhouse Square: Philadelphia
Plan a bicycle ride to brunch
See the city from new heights
Feel cobblestones beneath your pedals
Converse with others once you arrive at your destination
Freelance your life

Amicable Engagement

SHARED FORGIVENESS

Feel the whisk of the Seaport: Boston
Walk on a brisk fall day
Wear a new sweater and scarf
Share a glove with a friend

Soothing Saturday

REFLECTIONS OF SELF

Steep chamomile tea while wrapped in a warm blanket
Sit in front of the ambient fireplace
View forever-changing colors
Pull out an old diary
Create a new one

Open House Sunday

RANDOM OLIVES FOR A FRUITFUL LIFE

SOULFUL MOMENTS

Listen to cotton-smooth Michael Franks
Cleaning house
Prop windows open
Wade in the nice subtle breeze
Think about painting your new life canvas
OWN *Super Soul Sundays* with Oprah

Risk Taking

CLOSURE OR SOFT OPENINGS

Call a family member who you have lost contact with
Just to say hello
Leave the drama back where you left it
Make amends by your actions

Intertwined Palates

KINESTHETIC MOVEMENTS

See Balanchine's *The Nutcracker*
See Alvin Ailey's *Revelations*
Explore polar opposites ... maybe not
Soothing to the soul

Let the Sunlight In

CAPTAIN OF YOUR SHIP

Take a sailing course in Marina Del Rey
Allow the sunbeam on your back
Yellow rays on your face
Navigate your journey
We are waiting to applaud your efforts

Draw Back the Curtain

SELF-IMPOSED HURDLES

Cancún ... Cancún
Oasis loves you
Get out of the white boxes
Dive into the blue ocean
Promote self-love
Give yourself a standing ovation
Celebrate clarity

Decipher What You Want

QUIET BREVITY

Aruba loves you
Open up to the "One Happy Island"
Stillness in the private moments
Observe prickly cacti
Awareness of the intersection of iguanas and pelicans

Empowerment x Empowerment

PERSONAL POWER

Learn how to say "no" again
More importantly, learn how to say "yes" more frequently
Reclaim and discard

Self-Exploration

FREEDOM

Take more pictures
Build a selfie portfolio
Capture random highlights and encounters in your life
Do you remember the last time you saw yourself?
Reflective memories
Post Wildly on Instagram

Free Expression

NO HANDS

Plan a rustic autumn getaway
Travel around aimlessly in the Town Centre
Hint: Newton, Mass.
Grab Mystic Pizza on your way back down or up the highway

Build a Clean Slate

OWN LIFE

Turn off the news for a week or two
Engage in digital detox
See what news you can create
What's on your canvas?

Revel in the Moment

PASSIONATE VITALITY

La Marca … La Marca
Indulge in pan-roasted veggies with halibut
rubbed in garlic olive oil
Partake in five-star conversations
La Marca … La Marca … La Marca
Unleash your intuitive spirit

Try Love Again

GLIMPSE OF SELF

Found Dornfelder late in life
Sweet like baby back ribs
Succulent touches
Supple appetite
Traveling along the way

Live a Prism Life

MINIMALISTIC LIVING

Silver linings
White mortar
Red brick
Yellow windows
Blue skies
Red airplanes
Green elevated pedestrian scores
Forgo the stainless steel persona

Indulge in Oceanic Healing

THOUGHTFUL MOMENTS

Hit the beach at least once a year
Keep your beach tag
Cherish your memento #64
Live tranquilly
Thrive fruitfully

Live Out of Bounds

RANDOM OLIVES FOR A FRUITFUL LIFE

ALTERED PERSPECTIVE

Slowly drive to New Hope
Breathe in winding roads, vast river, and scenic foliage
Sit at the familiar Cuban Havana
Pushing the limits

Give Yourself Permission

AERIAL VIEW

Catch a midday movie
Sit at the top
Pink Floyd's "The Great Gig in the Sky" is the limit
Future to the moon and back
Empower yourself through Beyonce's "Superpower"
Mend inner fences

Introspective Moments

SIGH OF RELIEF

Walk to a local coffee shop
Wear your knitted hat
Frost leaving your breath
Get in touch

Energize Your Locomotive Emotions

RANDOM OLIVES FOR A FRUITFUL LIFE

SPONTANEITY OVER RISK

Take a train
Metro-North
People watch from the restaurant balcony
Listen to the chatter and movement
Tell the one you are with how you feel

Exhale Now

VICTORY BREATHS

Dance to "French Kiss"
Like you have never danced
Feel the vibe
Feel the bass
Release ... release ... release

Be Your Vibrant Self

CATHARTIC SENSORY

Rent a vintage convertible
Drive as far as you can on a tank of gas
Stop at a few consignment shops
Pilfer through wholesome goodness
Let go of your baggage

Music Heals All Wounds

REJUVENATION

Speaking of vinyl: DJ Rich Medina and DJ Rashida
Explore the world tour in your living room
Open your ears to the explosion
Allow vibrant moments of letting it all go

Reflective

BENCHMARK

Roam back to your college campus
See the change
Measure your growth one brick at a time
Prosperity

Cross Over to the Other Side

ELEVATED TRANSCENDENCE

Betsy has been good to me
Ben has been Frank
GW has watched me grow
Building bridges to open pathways
To the next ... beyond
Celebrate motorcades and victory brigades

Make New Friends

CONNECTIVITY

Game of life
Strong-willed or fortunate
Who's on your battleship?
Be selective

Life Is Worth Living

BARRICADED WALLS

Pain to my existence:
Episodic
Epidemic
Pandemic

Tantrums almost taste like red rum
Healing is the only option
Press #1

Increase Your Limit

RANDOM OLIVES FOR A FRUITFUL LIFE

ENCOURAGED BOUNDARYLESSNESS

Ride canary scooters in Rehoboth
Witness white sands, dark green smoothies,
and parrots that are purple
Be the unthinkable, question the unthinkable,
and do the unthinkable
Touch fluid layers of:
Empowerment
Encouragement
Adaptability

Reach

Expect People to Change

SERUM OF TRUTH

Brace for impact
Guard your grill
Know your friends
Better than your enemies

Begin to See Your Authentic Self

MEDITATIVE BLISS

The stillness of your brainwaves
Heightened acuity on your internal GPS
Believe in the cadence of your heartbeat
Internal healing brings you closer
to the one you are hiding from
Life is a cinematic flick in color or b/w
Even when you are just *Being Mary Jane*
Touch the 20/20 peripheral vision
Earplugs needed for your favorite *Ally McBeal* song
Moments of clarity
Rest your spirit daily
Contribute random olives

Philocaly

FLOWING VIBRATIONS OF GRATITUDE

It shows in all of your expressions and gratitude for life ...
The path that you walk so graciously ...
with love, inspiration, and grace ...
Inspiring the virtual masses around you
forever, with savory beauty ...
Your magic wand gives us sprinkly dust
Touches the window to our souls ...

Made in the USA
Middletown, DE
08 February 2021